Mississippi Map Turtle

Mississippi Map Turtle
Owner's Manual

Mississippi Map Turtle breeding, where to buy, types, care, temperament, cost, health, handling, diet, and much more included!

By: Lolly Brown

Copyrights and Trademarks

Disclaimer and Legal Notice

Foreword

Out of all reptiles that can be cared for as pets, turtles are the most loved and most popular. What's not to like? Turtles may not be cuddly at all, but they are exceedingly cute. Their facial expressions are charming, their shell patterns are very attractive, and their movements and habits are very gentle. Moreover, turtles are generally easy to care for. Even though different turtle species have different care requirements—diet, shelter, habitat, etc.—all turtles have a long life span and you have to commit yourself to consistently care for your turtle in the long haul. But rest assured it's going to be one great adventure!

If you want to take care of an exotic Mississippi map turtle or two, or you already have are a pet turtle owner and want to enhance your pet caring skills, then consider this book your turtle parenting tutorial. Read on about the history, biological information, husbandry, temperament, health and medical requirements, caring needs, and other pertinent information about the Mississippi map turtle.

Table of Contents

Introduction 1

Chapter One: Basic Biological Information 2

   Appearance 3

   Size 5

   Gender and Lifespan 6

   Care Level 6

   Diet and Feeding 7

   Health 7

   Behavior and Temperament 8

   Reproduction 9

   Protection 10

   Perils 10

   Ecology 11

Chapter Two: Turtle Care Sheet 12

   Feeding Your Pet Map Turtle 13

   Habitat 16

      Basking Platform 18

   Temperature and Light 19

   Water Care 21

   Handling 22

   Hatchlings in Enclosures 24

Special Care for Hatchlings 26

Multiple Turtles Together 29

Keeping Your Mississippi Map Turtle Happy 30

    Home Sweet Home 30

Have Regular Exercise 33

Prevent Odors from Your Pet Turtles 36

Chapter Three: Health Care and Medical Attention:
What to Do When Your Turtle Gets Sick 38

Finding a Good Herpetologist 40

General Health Issues 41

    Salmonella 42

    Pneumonia 43

    Respiratory Infections 44

    Coughing Up Stuff 44

    Crooked Swimming 45

    Inability to Submerge 45

    Septicemia 46

    Mouth Rot 47

    Prolapse 47

    Stunted Growth 49

    Lack or Loss of Appetite 49

    Not Swimming 51

Not Basking... 52

Sleeping a Lot 52

Burns, Bites, Cuts and/or Scratches 53

Eyes and Ears Problems 54

Shell and Skin Problems.. 57

Chapter Four: Fun Facts and Myths................................ 60

Fun Turtle Facts... 61

Myths Surrounding Turtles... 65

Chapter Five: Mississippi Map Turtle Laws and Regulations
.... 72

Map Turtle Laws 74

Taking a Wild Turtle Home as a Pet 76

Chapter Six: Petting and Training Your Mississippi Map
Turtle... 78

Chapter Seven: What to Do in Different Turtle Situations .. 86

Turtle Adoption.. 87

Moving to a New Place 88

Can't Take Care of Your Turtle Anymore? 90

Photo Credits 92

References 93

Introduction

There are about 270 species of turtles and pet options can be overwhelming. Map turtles are one of the most well-liked pet turtles, as they are not so expensive, easy to acquire and not too difficult to maintain. Additionally, the Mississippi Map Turtle is one of those types that are best suited to live with people, especially for novice turtle pet parents. Named for its markings that look like a map, the Mississippi map turtle can be found in most bodies of water located in the Gulf States all the way to the Valley of Mississippi. Mississippi map turtles rarely stay in creeks and farm ponds. Instead, they bask in rivers, streams and lakes.

When you decide to take Mississippi map turtles as pets, you need to make sure that they are provided with excellent water quality because they prefer to stay in water. You should also provide a floating item for them to climb on and laze around in the sun.

The female Mississippi map turtle is usually larger than the male ones. On the average, Mississippi map turtles are medium-sized turtles but females can grow up to 10 inches into adulthood while males can grow up to 5 to 6 inches. This adorable turtle has dark green-brown or grey-brown skin and a light olive green shell. The Mississippi map turtle's shell has an uncommon elevated middle ridge that you won't usually see in aquatic turtles. It also has noticeable, delicate black markings around the circumference of its shell.

The Mississippi map turtle is primarily carnivorous — it loves to feast on different kinds of small prey, both dead and alive. You can give it shrimp, mealworms, snails, earthworms, crickets, crayfish, smelts, and guppies. It will also enjoy commercial turtle food and vegetables like lettuce.

Owning and taking care of turtles is not the same as taking care of dogs or cats—but it will surely be an extraordinary learning experience. While you can't cuddle or play fetch with your turtle, you will be fascinated with its behaviors and the way it interacts with you. Caring for a pet such as the Mississippi map turtle will inspire you to learn different characteristics, sociability, specific needs, environmental requirements and other interesting information about turtles.

Another plus factor of taking care of the Mississippi map turtle is that it won't take up a lot of space. If you live in a small apartment in the city, taking care of cats, dogs or a bird, won't be a good option. You want something that you can place in a fairly small cage or aquarium. Don't worry, even small pets can give you the same level of companionship, joy and love that larger pets offer. Like they say, good things can be found in small packages.

One of the most promising advantages of having a Mississippi map turtle for a pet is that it doesn't need to be walked. They just require a bit of gentle handling in order to socialize. You can't mishandle them, though, as they will be stressed. You might find it funny, but turtles think they will become soup when they are being held. You will learn more about proper socialization with your pet turtle in the next chapters of this book. If you have a busy schedule, having a turtle will work for you.

Most reptiles, birds and small mammals like hamsters or gerbils are flexible when it comes to their owner's busy schedules and won't demand much time out of their cage for daily interaction. Furthermore, people who have allergies to dander, fur or feathers can still experience the satisfaction and delight of taking care of pets by getting one with no hair on its skin. Yes, the Mississippi map turtle is the perfect choice for them.

While most people don't want to get a pet for fear of becoming too attached to it only to be saddened by its loss, you won't have the same problem when you own a turtle. No pet lives forever, but turtles live a very, very long time even in captivity. When taken care of properly, given the right diet, housed appropriately and given great medical attention when needed, your Mississippi map turtle can live to its full lifespan of 30 to even 50 years. The potential to enjoy your pet's company for a long time is appealing and can be considered a blessing. Given the longevity of your pet turtle, you should consider if you have the finances, lifestyle and time to take care of it responsibly.

Mississippi map turtles are very endearing pets that are easy to care for when given a good environment to thrive. They make very interactive, fascinating and loving companions that may even outlive you!

It's a huge commitment, when you decide to bring home a Mississippi map turtle for a pet, but the if you're up for the challenge, then you will enjoy a big payout. You can be the best turtle parent there is and you can start today!

Introduction

Chapter One: Basic Biological Information

About 13 subspecies of map turtles are officially recognized and the Mississippi map turtle belongs to the aquatic false map turtle subspecies (Scientific name: *Graptemyspseudogeographica kohni*).

Joseph Gustave Kohn first discovered and gathered the foremost species of Mississippi map turtles in Louisiana. Though they are not native to it, the Mississippi map turtles inhabit the Mississippi Valley. They can be found along the stretches of water in Texas, Illinois, Iowa, Nebraska and other surrounding states of the Mississippi River. They love the moving, open waters of rivers, lakes, and streams, abundant vegetation and sunny places.

While they dislike isolated creeks and ponds, they will submerge in the water when they feel a disturbance in the area. That is why they tend to become slightly aggressive when taken out of their natural habitat.

The Mississippi turtles got its name from the Mississippi River—a long stretch of water from Louisiana to Minnesota. They are often nicknamed as "saw back" because their shells are raised and have a saw-like manifestation or carapace. They are also commonly called map turtles. The juvenile maps are called gray backs.

Even if you visit the bodies of water where you live, there is little likelihood that you will see a wild map turtle. These unique, often heavy-jawed map turtles have a habit of being shy and secretive and they tend to draw away from the adoring public as soon as they become aware of trespassers in their habitat. Map turtles are a fairly interesting group of turtles, and possess a few distinctive characteristics compared to their water-dwelling counterparts.

Appearance

Map turtles have a specialized body form: an overturned, serrated carapace, and hefty, broad forelimbs, and paddle-like hind feet. Map turtles are highly evolved and distinctively adapted, resulting in specific requirements that need to be met whether they are in natural environments or captive habitats.

All map turtles have different patterns on their shells. Mississippi map turtles are so named because of the prominent map pattern that can be seen on their shell. Mississippi maps are the most striking of all aquatic turtles. Here is a further description of some of distinctive body parts of a Mississippi map turtle that you need to know:

Head – To easily identify a Mississippi map turtle, look at its head. You can tell a Mississippi map turtle apart from other map turtles by the striking yellow reverse-crescents that you can see under its eyes. The curved lines start from the uppermost part of the Mississippi map turtles head and runs along to the center, cleaving down at each side. Another distinctive feature that a Mississippi map turtle has is its solid round pupil and bright-colored eyes. They usually don't have any bars across their irises.

Carapace – (top of the shell). This is one of distinguishing features of a map turtle. The carapace is the elevation of black-tipped bumps that run along the turtle's spine, and the rough, pointy rear exterior edge. Mississippi maps have moderately prominent black-tipped protrusions. The color of the Mississippi map turtle's shells are either brown or olive with a combination of thin yellow circles or lines. The patterns on its shell often fade as the turtle matures or can be concealed by an overgrowth of algae on the shell.

Plastron – (bottom of the shell). The Mississippi maps lower shell, called plastron, is either light green in color with a mix of yellow or yellowish tan, and has light brown lines that look a lot like wood grain. These light lines run along the seams of the turtle's scales. The map turtle's plastron may also have dark patterns. These patterns can also fade over time.

Size

The Mississippi ma turtle is a medium-sized turtle but it can grow into large adults. Female adult Mississippi map turtles can span a length of 6 to 10 inches and are larger than males which, on the other hand, can grow up to 4 to 6inches. Male Mississippi map turtles have marginally longer nails on their forelegs and longer tails, and while females have shorter tails, they have larger bodies than the males. Females also have bigger jaws.

Turtle measurement is done using the Straight Carapace Length or SCL. It means the turtle is measured from the front of its carapace to its back in a straight line that goes above the turtle. The ridge of the carapace is disregarded as it can give inaccurate measurements. It's a lot like getting two bookends and placing one on each side of the turtle, then measuring the distance between those bookends.

Gender and Lifespan

It is not easy to tell the difference in gender of turtles. You can only tell when they get mature. Male Mississippi map turtles will have thicker and longer tails and their cloaca will be seen close to the end of the tail. Female Mississippi map turtles have smaller and thinner tails and their vent is closer to their bodies. You will also notice that males have a concave plastron—this is so the males can better climb on the female during mating. Females have a semi-pliable plastron when they have already laid eggs. Most map turtles are plain, but sometimes you will find a female map with an attractive carapace.

Like most turtles, the Mississippi map turtle has a long life span. It averages 20 to 30 years in captivity, but if well taken care of, it can live up to 50 years!

Care Level

When in captivity, Mississippi map turtles can stress easily and become quite nervous, making taking care of them quite a challenging task. It is important to only purchase or adopt a Mississippi map turtle from reputable sellers and not get them from the wild. It may not be easy but it is not impossible to be successful at keeping them as pets. Learn more about how to care for your Mississippi map turtle in the succeeding chapters about Mississippi map turtle care sheets.

Diet and Feeding

Because they are aquatic, Mississippi map turtles do everything while they are in the water. They swim, exercise and even eat! Most Mississippi maps, if not all, will only feed while they are in water. You may see them get their food from where you put it on land and drag it to the water to feed. Mississippi map turtles are omnivores—they eat both meat and plants. However, they are more carnivorous and may tend to overeat protein. You have to watch their diet because their shells can pyramid and they may become unhealthy when they take in too much meat. The Mississippi map turtle's diet should be balanced. Find out more about what kinds of food you can give your Mississippi map turtle in the next chapters.

Health

Mississippi map turtles are generally healthy and they rarely get sick, especially when they are cared for in a proper environment. You need to make sure that clean water is maintained because they thrive well in good quality water conditions. They also need adequate natural sunlight and sufficient UVB lighting inside the house. Otherwise, they can easily develop fungal and bacterial infections and a metabolic bone disease. Fungal infections will appear as grey blotches and could spread all over the turtle's carapace. Metabolic bone disease may also result in shell deformity. With proper lighting and clean water, you can prevent it from happening. And if your turtle has these issues, then it is important to get it to the vet immediately for treatment.

Make sure that your Mississippi map turtle's nails and beak are maintained at a good length. The nails and beak may require periodic trimming especially when your map turtle is not able to grind them down in their enclosure. Check for excessive growth in these areas as it can be caused by an underlying health concern that needs to be addressed. Other common health problems are discussed in length in another chapter of this book.

Behavior and Temperament

The Mississippi map turtle is known for being skittish. However, you may be lucky to find some turtles that are an exception to this. When in captivity, you will observe that the Mississippi map turtles love to swim and submerge themselves in water. They also love to bask in the sun (or UVB lighting). However, they will prefer to bask in an area that is near the water so they can easily jump in when they feel edgy. Generally, Mississippi maps are very friendly. The females are more dominant than the males and if you are thinking of having multiple map turtles, make sure that you limit the number of females you get.

The Mississippi map turtles are also very active and you will enjoy watching them move and go about. It is very interesting to observe how they interact with their community, and even you, as it grows accustomed to your presence. Because of this, and their striking appearance, they are very popular as pets.

Reproduction

Female Mississippi map turtles can lay multiple clutches of eggs every breeding season. A clutch can contain five to sixteen eggs, and even go up to 22. The eggs will hatch after 60 to 85 days, depending on the temperature. In captive breeding, male maps are usually produced at temperatures of 77° to 83° F while females are produced at higher temperatures of 88° to 95°F. Mixed genders can be produced from clutches at 83° to 88°F. When temperatures are changed during incubation periods, shell patterns can be altered and the Mississippi map turtles may look like other species.

Protection

Considered community animals, Mississippi map turtles are very sociable and stay in groups. They are conscious of their environments and when one turtle is wary and suddenly dives into the water, all of the turtles in the group will follow quickly. This is how they protect themselves. The Mississippi map turtle is generally timid and will rarely show aggression. Aggression among its community often occurs when males compete with each other over a female they want to mate, and, would you believe, when female maps sexually harass their male counterparts. When this is the case, the turtles should be separated in different enclosures.

Perils

Since they are always in hiding when they get nervous, little is known about map turtles. It is suspected that other kinds of turtles prey on their eggs and their young. Humans generally don't bother Mississippi map turtles except in areas where turtles as taken for food. However, human activity greatly affects them and their habitat. Boat propellers can injure turtles and pollution often makes them sick.

Ecology

The Mississippi map turtles hardly ever travel overland. They will only come out of the water when it is time to bask or lay eggs. These map turtles are also very sensitive to water conditions. When the waterways are polluted, the Mississippi map turtles can die. While they are often considered in the pet trade as "beginner's turtles", if you are not careful with the quality of water you provide, a Mississippi map turtle will not do well in captivity and die easily.

A lot of map turtles are on protection by CITIES (Convention of International Trade in Endangered Species) and cannot be harvested in the wild. It is a wise move by states to consider these turtles into special breeding programs to prevent extinction in the future. The Mississippi map turtle is one of the most popular and readily available turtles in the pet trade. They are quite robust and can be kept in captivity. They also o not grow as big as most slider turtles. While they are less social than most pet turtle options, they can be great pets once they get your trust. If you have a growing love for the Mississippi map turtles, read on to discover more facts on how to care for them properly.

Chapter Two: Turtle Care Sheet

Once you have decided that you will get a pet turtle, make sure that you don't get one from the wild. Mississippi map turtles, for instance, have great difficulty adapting to captivity even though they are known for their adaptability and resiliency. It is best to get a captive-bred Mississippi map turtle as they have already adjusted to captive conditions once they are hatched and they tend to be tamer. Additionally, there is less likelihood of the turtles harboring parasites when you get them from your local breeder or pet store. You don't want a pet that is a disease carrier. That said, you need to remember that every turtle specie has specific requirements and care needs, from diet to housing to temperatures to health care.

In this chapter you will find detailed instructions and advice on how to care for your Mississippi map turtle so that it can live a long and healthy life.

Feeding Your Pet Map Turtle

As with every animal, a balanced diet is of utmost importance. Your Mississippi map turtle is an omnivore—it will like to eat meat from small animals as well as different kinds of leafy vegetables. You can get nutritionally-balanced turtle food in the form of pellets from your local pet store, too. Make sure that you supplement your turtle's diet with low-fat proteins and vitamin-rich greens such as dandelion leaves, spinach, romaine lettuce, escarole, red leaf, parsley, endive, kale and other dark greens.

When it comes to protein, you will know which kinds of meat your pet Mississippi map turtle prefers according to its gender. Female maps have bigger jaws and would love to eat slightly bigger prey such as clams and snails. Male maps will enjoy small fish, mealworms, tiny crustaceans, mollusks, and aquatic insects. Make sure that you don't give your turtles live mealworms as they might injure your turtle. Your turtles will also eat dead small fish, so they won't have a hard time catching live ones. Map turtles can also eat crickets and blood worms.

Do not feed your turtle with snails or crustaceans that you get from the wild — they may be carrying parasites or worms that can harm your turtles. You can give your Mississippi map turtle finely chopped fresh apple pieces — but you can only give them as a treat, not as everyday food.

If you get a young turtle, keep in mind that it will have a very big appetite and you should feed it daily. However, you should feed it with just enough to prevent it from being hungry. If you place too much food, it won't stop from gorging itself.

Recommended Feeding Schedule

Age	Frequency	Diet
Hatchlings	Once a day	Turtle pellet and live foods
Juvenile	4 to 5 times a week	Live foods and vegetation
Adult	3 to 4 times a week	Live foods and vegetation

You will be surprised to know that turtles can actually "beg" for food. When you pass by their home, you will notice your pet looking longingly at you or be close to where they know the food shelf is. It can be hard to resist those adorable yes, but you should. As much as you love to see your pet turtle feed, never give it too much food. To determine how much you should give, check how much your turtle can consume within 4 to 5 minutes and use that as a basis. This will help you avoid overfeeding and eventual obesity and fatty liver disease.

Remember, everything in excess is never good. You should adjust the food intake or feeding schedule according to your pet turtle's growth rate. Tip: your turtles can have an all-you-can-eat romaine lettuce no matter what its age is, because romaine is mostly water.

Mississippi maps will feed in the water, so you should place your leaves in the water or clip them to the side of their aquarium using rubber suction. You can also put the leaves and protein on their basking site, in an area near the water.

If you want to keep the quality of your water clean — which is very important to the Mississippi map turtles — you can use a separate feeding tank, especially if you have the space and resources. This will help you clean up food wastes easily and prevent the spread of salmonella which is harmful for you.

Your Mississippi map turtle will also need a daily calcium supplement that you can sprinkle on their food. Provide your pet with a cuttlefish bone that it can gnaw on. Keep it away from the water so that it will remain dry. You can also give your map turtle the appropriate multi-vitamin supplement once or twice a week.

On the other hand, your turtle may go through a hibernation period and will stop eating for a period of time. If you feel that it is not hibernating and its lack of appetite is a sign of illness, do not hesitate to get a checkup with a veterinarian.

Habitat

The Mississippi map turtles will almost always swim. And when they're not swimming, they will stay in the basking area and lounge. You will find a variety of tanks specially made for map turtles in your local pet store.

It is important to set up your aquarium meticulously so that your Mississippi map turtle will grow well in captivity. An aquarium or tank should be large enough for your map turtle to swim in freely. Baby turtles are about 1 ½ to 2 inches in size. Since they don't grow too big, a 25-gallon aquarium will be enough for a male. If you are getting a female map turtle, you will need at least a 75-gallon tank because females grow larger.

Get a good filtration system to clean your water regularly, keep it clear and prevent odors. Purchase something that is larger than the recommended filter. A submersible filter like canister filters or cascade internal filters will constantly run and provide aeration to the water portion of your enclosure.

The tank or aquarium should have a minimum height of 300mm as well as a dock and ramp placed in such a way that so that turtle can have enough space to swim and get out. A good guide to getting the right size of your aquarium or tank is the ratio of ten gallons to every each of your turtle. You will need a sizable aquarium if you are planning to put more than one turtle in it. It is better to get a bigger one than having one that is way too small.

Make sure you put your aquarium or tank in a safe place, especially if you have children or other pets at home. They can reach out or jump in and make the aquarium fall and cause injury. Keep the enclosures away from tables and edge of shelves. Additionally, secure any cords and tubes from heaters, lights, and filters.

In the past, keepers were not really providing sanitary living conditions for turtles. They used to keep turtles in turtle bowls where the water was not filtered and was only changed when it smelled foul.

The turtles had to live in, feed and swim in the same water where they discharge their feces. This is why the turtle bowls were often called death bowls. Turtles get sick and there was always the risk for spreading salmonella. It's a good thing so much has changed for the better.

Basking Platform

Setting up a basking platform is very important if you want your Mississippi map turtle to enjoy its new home. All map turtles bask zealously—it is good for their health and well-being. Basking helps raise the metabolism of a turtle. In effect, the immune system is bolstered and digestion is facilitated. After a good swim, your Mississippi map turtle needs to fry its skin completely and it does so by basking. The dead skin and old scutes will shed as they bask. If basking conditions are poor, your pet turtle can suffer from shell rot, skin infections and abscesses in its ears.

You will also need a good flat surface for a basking site. You can even get two. These aquatic turtles love to bask in the light. Your basking site should be non-toxic and non-abrasive and should be able to support your pet turtle's weight. Also, map turtles like vegetation so it is good to put live aquatic plants in your tank. You can even get fake ones but make sure they are not sharp so your pet won't get scratched or cut.

Use secure natural and artificial structures such as driftwood, shell, small log, smooth rocks or plastic basking docks. Set them up in a way that is both visually appealing and helpful to your pet. Make sure to provide an area where your pet turtle can hide when it needs to, like a cave or tunnel. When you set-up these structures, bear in mind that you want your turtle to be comfortable in maneuvering around the area and safe from drowning. Make sure that the basking platform is big enough to allow a variety of temperatures.

Temperature and Light

The Mississippi map turtle needs ample amounts of natural sunlight as well as specific UVB-lighting that is placed over the basking site or sites. You can place your enclosure in a spot where direct sunlight can reach your map turtle. However, while there is no substitute for actual, unfiltered sunlight that all living things need, sometimes you cannot create a perfect basking spot with natural sunlight. Besides, you also have to watch out for accidental overheating caused by direct exposure to sunlight. You can use a UVB light bulb set-up instead. In most pet stores, you can select from a plethora of suitable UV light bulbs that can synthesize the production of Vitamin D that your pet turtle needs.

This nutrient will help them absorb calcium for good shell development and healthy bones. Do not get UVA bulbs as they are inadequate and cannot synthesize Vitamin D. Make sure that your UVB lighting is not being blocked by glass or plastic so the turtles can get the right amount of light and heat. The UVB lighting should also be changed every 9 months to one year.

Mississippi map turtles don't require particularly warm temperatures but they will be more energetic and will feed better if the enclosure's temperatures are kept at 80 to 85 degrees Fahrenheit. If temperatures in the tank drop below the 60's, your Mississippi map turtle may become sluggish, stop eating well, or begin to go into hibernation.

The temperature over your turtle's basking site should range from 80 to 90 degrees Fahrenheit. The air inside the tank should be low to mid-80 degrees.

Water temperature is equally important. It should range from low to mid-70 degrees. You have to maintain the perfect temperature range within the whole habitat because Mississippi map turtles, like other species, will regulate their body temperature by swimming and basking. You will also need a regular light set with timer than will mimic the transition of day and night.

Water Care

Mississippi map turtles will almost always be in the water so it should be your priority as the pet owner to keep it warm and keep it clean. Turtles can be so messy because of their high protein diet. They will see the world as a big bathroom and there will be feces everywhere. Their life will be an ongoing cycle of feeding and discharging waste. You would need a strong filter and you will also have to clean the whole enclosure every quarter. Opt for a system than can filter an enclosure that is double the size of what you have. Invest in a small vacuum or siphon device that you can use to clean the enclosure. Get an aerator to improve the quality of your water.

The water should be treated and de - chlorinated as chlorine can harm your turtle's eyes. Also, hard water can cause mineral build up in your turtle's shell as well as ruin the biological pads in your water filter. You can use a water heater to keep your water warm enough for your turtle. Here's a good guide: 1 watt can warm 1 liter of water. If you have a large aquarium, you should get two half-strength water heaters and put them on both ends.

Handling

Most reptile pets, turtles included, carry salmonella and these bacteria can infect people who handle them. Salmonella infections can cause fever, abdominal cramps and diarrhea. Children and elderly can have complications when infected. This is why proper handling is important. Just because the turtle doesn't look sick doesn't mean that it can't infect you with the bacteria. They can shed it through their stool. When you are cleaning your enclosure or handling your pet Mississippi map turtle, make sure that you use sterile gloves or wash your hands before and after. Don't be scared of handling your pet, though. Just observe the simple precautions to prevent infection. Likewise, do not let children handle turtles without adult supervision so that they don't put the animals near their mouths and eyes.

Also, do not mix your pet maps with other pets with no supervision. Different kinds of animals should be kept separate because they may hurt each other or become food. For instance, a cat can scratch your pet map and it can cause serious harm. Here are some tips on how to properly handle or pick up a turtle.

- Never pick the turtle from the front as it will give them the opportunity to bite you when they become surprised or scared. Always pick it up from the back.

- Place your palm under the turtle's plastron, making sure the legs can touch the palm of your hand. Balance it safely on your hand by touching the shell with your other hand.

- Wear gloves when you pick them up because they tend to urinate every time they get handled.

- Do not touch a turtle's claws or legs.

- Put your turtle on a flat surface and not on the brinks of high surfaces. They won't know when they walk off the edge and fall. Their shells may be hard but they are not invincible. They can injure themselves from a fall.

- Check the temperature. If it is too cold, turtles won't want to interact and will withdraw into their shell when you try to touch them. When it's warm they will be more receptive.

- You can touch, pet, or pick up a turtle after it has basked or when it is lounging under a heat lamp.

- Make sure you understand how turtles communicate. They don't want any form of contact when they hiss, withdraw into their shells, make snapping gestures or sit motionless with mouths hanging open.

- Remember, avoid picking your turtle up when it's not needed.

Hatchlings in Enclosures

Even if you get a Mississippi map hatchling, your enclosure requirements should match that of an adult. Hatchlings are capable of swimming in deep waters, just as adults are. If you have very small hatchlings (about the size of a 50-cent piece) you can initially put in 8 inches of water which you should increase as time goes by, as your pet turtle grows. You should also put the same kind of lighting and heat. It is best to add plants to your hatchling enclosure, whether live or artificial as well as other items that protrude from the surface of the water, like smooth rocks and very small driftwood logs. Your hatchling will need these things to stay rest and hide in. Mississippi map hatchlings are very vulnerable and private and prefer a lot of cover. Make sure you keep your enclosure temperatures warmer than that of adults, as hatchlings are very sensitive and have a high mortality rate.

The following are examples of minimal supplies requirements for your Mississippi map hatchlings:

- **A 20-gallon (or larger) aquarium or turtle tank:** If you have the option to buy a turtle tank, then go for it, as it has a cutout on the side that will allow you to lace a small filter for about 2 1/5 inches of water. The hatchlings will need the filter when it is a few weeks old. Make certain that you put the tank on a surface that can support its weight even when gallons of water are added. You can buy a commercial stand or use any sturdy table. Consider the weight of the gravel and the water, which is about 8.5lbs/gallon, together.

- **Filtration system:** It can be a side filter when you have a small tank, then change it to a pond or canister filter as your pet turtles grow larger.

- **Thermometer:** to measure the temperatures in the enclosure.

- **Turtle pellets that have the appropriate size for your small pets:** Remember your Mississippi map turtle tends to swallow its food whole and you don't want it to choke.

- Fluorescent lighting
- UVB bulb
- Screen top (not the aquarium glass covers)
- Clamp lights
- A 60 to 75-watt bulb for heat
- A 200-watt turtle heater
- River pebbles
- Small aquatic plants
- Basking stand
- Other decorations and floating devices held by suction cups that your pet turtle can hook onto
- Turtle system for cleaning your tank and siphoning out or adding water

Special Care for Hatchlings

Turtles that have just been hatched will still have their egg tooth in their beak and their yolk sac dangling on their bellies. The yolk sac is what they were feeding on the whole time they were incubating and the egg tooth is what they used to break out of their egg shell. The egg tooth will eventually come out on its own and the sac will be absorbed by its body. Never ever try to remove the yolk sac as it will kill the hatchling. Once the yolk sac is taken up into the body, the plastron will have a noticeable split.

Don't worry; it doesn't have to be treated as it will heal on its own. If you are looking to buy a hatchling, don't worry about these things. Breeders will not peddle turtles until the yolk sac has been fully absorbed.

Hatchlings or baby turtles are very delicate. Their shells are still quite soft and can be damaged by too much handling. Should you need to pick the hatchling up, you should hold it lightly by the center point of its top shell using your thumb and finger then settle it on your palm. Use your other hand to support the sitting turtle to keep it from falling.

Your water should be pH neutral or alkaline to help the shell become stronger as it grows. pH neutral or alkaline water will also keep your baby Mississippi map turtle from acquiring fungal infections. A higher level pH in the water can stress the baby turtle and soften its shell. Hatchlings also don't like dirty water and are sensitive to pollution and changes in the water temperature and quality.

The water temperature should be warm at 80 degrees Fahrenheit and should never drop below 70 degrees or get higher than 85 degrees. When the water temperatures are too high, the babies can suffer from overheating. When the temperatures are too low, the babies won't eat and will be lethargic.

Frequent water change is the rule in taking care of map turtles and it is even more important in caring for hatchlings. Make sure to get a good filtration system that is suited to the depth of water allowed and keep the intake port away from the turtle's reach so it won't get stuck and drown. The water should be shallow at only about 2 to 2.5 to inches deep in the first weeks and can be increased to 3 inches or more in about four months, when the turtle is becoming active. When the turtles are six months old, they can go to any water depth.

It is important to provide things that a baby turtle can hold onto and rest in the midst of shallow water, such as fake plants, ramp, rock or dry land, so that it can have space to breathe. If there is no available thing it can latch on to, it will just tread in water and may experience difficulty.

It is also advisable to separate the babies from adult or larger turtles so they won't get scratched, bitten, drowned or overtaken by the big ones for food. It is good to have a number of feeding points in the enclosure if you are housing more than one hatchling.

Hatchlings and juvenile Mississippi map turtles should have their own basking areas with regulated temperatures of about 90 to 100 degrees Fahrenheit.

Multiple Turtles Together

If you are planning in getting more than one Mississippi map turtle, it is important to get a really big enclosure to avoid overcrowding. Keep your turtle populations to a minimum. More importantly, try not to put different species of turtles together. You should also avoid housing turtles of different sizes together as the bigger ones can be aggressive to the smaller ones or vice versa. It has been observed that small hatchlings will also be aggressive when it comes to feeding so they may bite other turtles in competition for food. You may need to add extra basking spots with the consideration of having all your turtles basking at the same time.

Turtles won't grow at the same time—some may develop faster than others. If this is the case, then make sure to separate smaller turtles from the bigger ones during feeding. Find the balance between overcrowding the map turtles' enclosure with the need to put additional aquatic plants such as duckweed, water hyacinth or water lettuce) to have a good level of oxygen. The aquatic plants will be a good hiding place for shy turtles that need to stay away from aggressive ones.

Keeping Your Mississippi Map Turtle Happy

So you're bringing home a Mississippi map turtle. It may take a lot of work to care for it, but it can be a very rewarding experience. Since your Mississippi map turtle will be with you for quite a long time, it is important to keep it happy and healthy.

Home Sweet Home

Earlier in this chapter, you learned about what kind of enclosure is best for your pet map, what size is fit until it reaches its potential mature size, and other necessary elements. Never forget, when it comes to turtle homes, size matters. You need to provide your pet turtle with lots and lots of space—for swimming, basking, exercising and playing. Your Mississippi map turtle will be unhappy when it feels that the space is too tight, crowded or crammed. The bigger the enclosure, the happier your pet turtle. Get one that is up to four times the potential length of your pet. Think about it, their home in the wild is a very large territory. Do your best to reflect that environment in your home habitat.

To make the tank a happy home, you can also build a beach. Aquatic turtles like the Mississippi map turtles not only love to spend time in water, they also like to stay on dry ground. A beach set-up will make them happy as they can do both of the things they love. Designing a beach habitat will also be a fun project and allow you to let your creative juices flowing. Just don't go overboard. Remember it is for your pet turtle, not you. Here are some tips:

- The water portion should be deeper than your turtle's shell width so that it can swim freely and be completely submerged.

- When you landscape the dry portion, make sure that it will be easy for your pet turtle to climb up or down from it to the water portion.

- Don't forget to make the basking platform comfortable as it is where your Mississippi map turtle will likely spend 10 to 12 hours every day.

Just as you want a clean home for yourself, your turtles need it, too. If you do not clean your enclosure, both your pet turtle and its home will stink, making it undesirable to see and increasing the risk for health issues. Make sure you also clean your turtle, especially as algae will tend to build on its shell. Don't forget to wash your hands before and after handling your pet turtle.

When your turtle gets back from the store to its own enclosure in your home, give it time to settle down. During the first three days or so, it will probably just look around and get the feel of its new surroundings. After a while, it will come out and do things that are naturally to it, like swimming and basking. If, however, you notice the following symptoms, then have a veterinarian check your pet turtle as it may not be a simple case of homesickness or inadaptability:

- Minimal drinking or eating
- Hiding all of the time
- Loss of weight
- Swelling of joints
- Discharge from mouth, eyes or nose
- Discoloration of skin

Part of the turtle enjoying its home is your company that goes with it. Even if Mississippi map turtles are generally shy and nervous, they can possess different personalities. If your pet map is the sociable kind, it will love to be handled. You can pet its shell, head or chin. Make sure that your pet is allowing you to do it. If not, make sure you keep handling to a minimum. Most of them do not like to be lifted up, as they feel safe when their feet are on the ground. But handling becomes necessary when checking them for health issues, playing, exercise, and for enclosure cleaning. Never, ever put your turtle on its back. It's not funny and your pet turtle will become afraid and stressed. Similarly, do not force your pet map out of its shell for whatever reason, and do not grab its tail. Mississippi map turtles like to be lifted at its midsection. Don't pick it up by its legs. Don't worry about handling; you will get the hang of it. The key factor is to handle it with love and you can never go wrong.

Have Regular Exercise

Even though turtles are slow moving and they are hard on the outside, it doesn't mean that they can't exercise like other pets do. In fact, they need a bit of movement to stay healthy.

Even if you have bought a relatively large enclosure to give your turtle lots of space to move around, your Mississippi map turtle will still need extra room to play and exercise. This turtle is particularly active and can cover a lot of ground, even with its cumbersome body. Let your turtle play or walk outside its enclosure. It is important that there are no other pets in the house, such as a dog or cat, which can accidentally bite or hurt your turtle. If you have other people in the house, let them know that your pet turtle is taking a walk.

Provide barriers so you can limit the location of your pet's exercise. All of these precautions will prevent any fatal accidents.

To help your Mississippi map turtle exercise in its enclosure, put live fish in as a game. Your pet turtle will enjoy the hunt and the effort to swim and catch its prey is a great exercise. The Mississippi map will enjoy hunting mosquito fish, red minnow, young goldfish and guppies. You can also put live insects such as wax worms, grasshoppers, beetle larva, crickets, caddis flies and mayflies to keep your turtle on its toes while feeding. Tadpoles, small frogs, clams, black worms and earthworms are also good food for your pet turtle.

Go to your local pet store and get your Mississippi map turtle some toys. Your turtle will enjoy playing and even though it is often better not to handle them constantly, you can enjoy watching them play. An empty shell or a small toy raft will be great for sliding down. Some games you can play with your pet turtle will require you to use food or treats. You can build an obstacle course using materials in your turtle's habitat such as plants, sticks, stones and water pits. To encourage your turtle to go through it, place a treat at the end. You can also play "find-the-treat". Hiding live insects in your turtles' enclosure will give it a challenge to hunt for the reward.

You can teach your Mississippi map turtle to feed from your hand. This can happen when you establish a connection with your pet, which of course can take some time and patience. There needs to be some kind of familiarity and developed trust before your turtle will climb on your hand to eat. To start, try placing a small piece of fruit on your hand near your fingertips and slowly put your hand near your turtle and try not to move too much. If it likes the fruit, and gets it from your hand, then you can try again, this time placing the fruit on your palm, so the turtle will crawl further. If it still likes to do so, you can move the fruit up to your wrist so your pet will crawl on your hand in order to get it.

Always be patient with your turtle. It won't always easily do the tricks or play games with you but don't be sad. Moreover, make sure that the activities you plan will not stress your pet turtle too much. Unlike with other pets, you cannot play or exercise with your turtle everyday.

Prevent Odors from Your Pet Turtles

This will keep both you and your turtle happy. No one wants to stink. And while a wet turtle won't smell as bad as a wet dog, it can still be unpleasant and can be a sign of impending illness. Bad odors can usually come from rotting or stale food as well as unclean water. Here are some tips:

- Monitoring the ration of your turtle size to its tank size is important. Growing turtles produce more waste than you expect and a small tank will be unhygienic. It will smell quickly and cause your turtle to smell bad, too.

- Having a regular cleaning regime is important. You don't have to wash, vacuum and disinfect your enclosure every week. Chances are great that you will have to clean your aquarium at least once a week to remove uneaten food and feces. You can use tongs to do so. To siphon debris from the water portion, you can use a bucket and gravel cleaner. If your turtle's water area is a bowl, you should change the water every day. If it is a large tank, you can do partial water changes once a week. Compared to fish or amphibian aquarium cleaning, you can remove more water at a time from a turtle's enclosure. This is because turtles can breathe air and have waterproof skins. If your Mississippi map turtle lives in a terrarium, then you should clean the whole tank. Should your tank still stink even though you have done a thorough cleaning routine, then increase the number of times you change the water or increase the frequency of cleaning every week.

- Choose a bigger filtration system as it will reduce smells more efficiently. Also, change your filter media regularly.

- Do not use commercial cleaners. Some people think that they can mask the smells by using deodorizers or scented products. While they may smell better, they can be deadly to your pet turtle. Likewise, do not spray air freshener in the same room as your turtle's enclosure. If you need to use a disinfectant, get one that it is reptile-safe and make sure to rinse the enclosure thoroughly.

- If you feel that you still don't like the smell of your turtle's tank inside your home, you can move it to an enclosed backyard pond. Make sure that the climate outside your home is suitable for your Mississippi map turtle.

Chapter Three: Health Care and Medical Attention: What to Do When Your Turtle Gets Sick

When you buy a turtle for a pet, or adopt one, you make a promise to provide it with everything it needs. Taking very good care of your Mississippi map turtle will ensure that it stays healthy and lives a long life. Make sure you are familiar with the care sheet and to know exactly how to meet your turtle's requirements diligently. However, like other pets, turtles also do get sick and they can require medical attention. This chapter will discuss a short list of common turtle problems, symptoms and what you need to do in case your turtle goes under the weather, so you won't panic.

As you go over the list of common health concerns of Mississippi map turtles, you will find that there are always two things that come recommended: raising the temperature of their habitat and obtaining qualified assistance from a herpetologist. Turtles are ectothermic, which means their bodies will absorb the temperature of their surroundings. This is the reason you may have to adjust water, ambient air and basking temperatures.

Turtles will function better when the temperatures are brought up. This will also boost their immune system, as heat will kill any infection that is in their bodies. However, similar to humans, too high temperatures can also cause health problems or even kill your pet turtle. Should the situation call for you to raise the temperature of your Mississippi turtle's habitat, remember the following rule of thumb: raise water temp up to 5°F and raise air and basking temp to no more than 10°F. If you raise the temperatures higher than these, you may cause more harm than good to your pet.

First things first: make it a priority to find a herpetologist in your area—you don't want just an ordinary veterinarian, you want someone who is very familiar with turtles in particular and one who has experience working with Mississippi map turtles. It is always good to have one on your phone list, should the need to see one arise. Medical conditions of turtles are rarely severe; most of them don't require professional treatment. But when you are in doubt about your how your turtle is doing, consult a herpetologist.

Finding a Good Herpetologist

It is not easy to find a qualified turtle vet. Not all veterinarians are well-versed in taking care of turtles. And you can't just find one in a phone book. They don't come by the dozens, unlike vets for dogs and cats. Check out the state-by-state listing from the NYTTS and ATP to find vets that have a good reputation and experience with all things turtle.

While there is no set standard to finding out if a veterinarian truly knows about how to take care of turtles. Do your research to get all the information you need as well as questions you may have regarding medical care and husbandry, then go for a visit. Call or visit the vet to have a talk with him or her. Don't bring your Mississippi map turtle with you on your first visit as the vet may start to check it up and charge you for consultation. It is important to have a basic knowledge of pet turtle care so that the vet won't snowball you with information and make a big deal about knowing so much. Here's a tip: a great sign that your vet (and his/her attendants) do know about turtles is that they can give its scientific name. Another sign is when he or she can tell the gender of your turtle accurately. You can also check if that vet has given you right information by going to the TurtleForum.com and post a query—you will likely get a response from experienced keepers about the things the vet said and if he or she is right on track.

General Health Issues

Here is a list of common medical situations and symptoms that you may observe in your Mississippi map turtle. Should you experience any of these health issues, make sure you quarantine your pet from other turtles or other pets in your home.

- Salmonella
- Pneumonia
- Respiratory Infections (Coughing/Sneezing)
- Coughing up Stuff
- Crooked Swimming
- Inability to Submerge
- Septicemia
- Mouth Rot
- Prolapse

- Stunted Growth
- Lack or Loss of Appetite
- Not Swimming
- Not Basking
- Sleeping a Lot
- Bites, Cuts, Burns and Scratches
- Eyes and Ears Problems
- Shell and Skin Problems

Salmonella

This is one of the main issues that people are often afraid of—turtles carrying salmonella. You need to understand that practically all animals carry and can transmit salmonella, in spite of the good care they are given and quality of life they have. Yes, a turtle's gut flora has salmonella and it spends its whole life lives having it. You can live with a turtle that has salmonella—the important thing is that the salmonella isn't transmitted to you! There are two important key factors that will help prevent you and others in your home from getting infected and poisoned with salmonella: good personal hygiene and excellent habitat conditions for your pet turtle.

Always wash your hands before and after handling your Mississippi map turtle. Use anti-bacterial soap. Keep your turtle's living conditions sanitary. Clean out any plant waste as well as feces—salmonella will spread faster in such materials. Change your turtle's water every so often. Clean up the tank regularly. It doesn't have to be sterile, just clean. Also, it is not recommended that your turtles roam freely around your home. If you maintain cleanliness and proper hygiene, you will avoid catching salmonella and get to enjoy your pet turtle.

Pneumonia

Turtles in captivity almost always die of pneumonia. As a pet owner, you can't diagnose it right away and your Mississippi map turtle may either be exhibiting symptoms for several months or not show any signs at all until near death. One of the most common signs is sighing. Another sign is coughing up stuff, such as lung tissue. However, instead of being scared or worried that your pet turtle might catch pneumonia, just make sure that you maintain preventive measures:

- Based on your Mississippi map care sheet, keep your ambient air, water, and basking temperatures in a comfortable degree to meet your pet's requirements. Often, when the ambient air temperature falls below the water temperature, your pet turtle may develop pneumonia.

- Make sure that your turtle is kept away from open windows that can bring in draft. This is especially important during winter.

Respiratory Infections

Don't be surprised, turtles cough and sneeze! When they do, it shows that they have a respiratory infection. When your Mississippi map turtle is submerged under water, coughing will appear like a convulsive shock. It can also look like a large, long yawn while your turtle is twitching its head. When it is basking, a turtle's cough will sound like a croak. A turtle's sneeze sounds like chirping. When you see or hear your turtle cough or sneeze, make sure you quarantine it at an environment with a temperature raised by 5°. Then consult your herpetologist for required medication.

Coughing Up Stuff

If you notice your Mississippi map turtle spitting up or coughing up something other than food during mealtimes, then you should give it immediate attention. When eating a lot of food too fast, your pet turtle may spew up their food, especially if they come in large portions. However, it should be cause for alarm when the material they cough up is white and appears to be shed skin. This could mean that your Mississippi map turtle has lung infection, pneumonia or stomatitis. Quarantine the turtle and raise temperatures by 5°. Make sure your pet turtle gets veterinary attention immediately.

Crooked Swimming

Listing, or swimming in a crooked manner, is another cause for concern. You will notice that your turtle is swimming crookedly when one of its sides is lower than the other as it reels in the water. Crooked swimming happens when one of your Mississippi map turtle's lungs is filled with more fluid compared to the other, or the fluid is in only one of the turtle's lungs. It can also be a sign of pneumonia.

Inability to Submerge

Turtles love to swim underwater and if you observe your Mississippi map turtle is having a hard time to get submerge, you may be looking at one of two health issues: respiratory infection or gastrointestinal problem. Usually, gastrointestinal problems occur after your pet has taken a regimen of antibiotics. The turtle's gut flora is unstable and it cannot digest food properly, leading to a rather profuse release of gas. However, when the turtle's back end keeps floating even as its front end is trying to go down the water and this condition continues, the situation could be severe and you should consult your turtle's veterinarian. As with other medical problems, make sure you quarantine your sick turtle and raise the habitat's temperature by 5°.

Septicemia

Turtles can suffer blood poisoning. Toxins can enter your pet turtle's body and can be quite deadly. If your Mississippi map turtle is suffering from septicemia, you should take it to the herpetologist immediately. There is no home remedy that can help. So when you notice that your turtle is withdrawn into its shell for long periods of time, and basking or floating in the same manner, then you should be concerned. Other symptoms that your turtle has septicemia include swelling of the skin, reddish tint in the skin, inflammation of the eyes and vomiting.

Mouth Rot

An infection in your Mississippi map turtle's mouth can either be viral or bacterial. Untreated mouth rot can be deadly and also highly contagious. Some mouth infections are caused by chlamydial organisms and E. coli bacteria as well as herpes-type viruses. When your turtle has a mouth infection and is also coughing up or spitting, it can also have stomatitis in its throat. It is important that your turtle is quarantined in a clean environment and given immediate veterinarian attention.

Prolapse

Prolapses can be intestinal or penile. Usually, Mississippi map turtles can get intestinal prolapse by ingesting gravel. When the ingested gravel is being pushed out of the turtle's digestive system, it can get lodged in the intestines. As the turtle's body forces it out, part of the intestinal tract goes with it. Usually, it can repair itself after the feces is expelled. However, when it doesn't repair, you must remove your pet turtle from its environment. If you have other turtles with it, they may bite the prolapse, thinking it is food. This can seriously injure your pet or even cause death.

Make sure you put your injured turtle in a clean container and layer the prolapse with honey or dry, granulated sugar. The coating will reduce the swelling and help the self-repair process. If you can, immobilize your pet turtle so that it won't drag, cut, or step on the prolapse as it walks. If the prolapse won't go back on its own, you can very gently push it back to the vent once the swelling is gone. If you don't feel like you can do a good job at it, bring your pet turtle to the vet so the intestines can be returned properly. A purse string can also be sutured so the prolapse won't happen again.

A penile prolapse, on the other hand, can be a secondary condition to another health issue. Again, make sure that you separate the injured turtle from others in the habitat so its condition doesn't get worse. When your turtle with a penile prolapse appears to be displaying itself, don't be worried. The turtle can swat or kick at its penis while it is retracting, until it goes back.

You can assist your pet turtle this way: make sure your hands are clean and use sterile gloves, lubricate your turtle's penis with KY jelly, then gently push the organ back.

Or you can layer the organ with honey or dry, granulated sugar to help reduce the swelling. The penis will retract on its own or you can gently push it back if it doesn't go back naturally. Again, if you don't feel confident or comfortable doing this, go to a vet. You don't want to cause further damage. Some prolapse conditions may require topical medication then suturing.

Stunted Growth

As with most animals, not all Mississippi map turtles will develop at the same rate. However, their growth should not stop. Some factors that cause this include improper diet, inadequate lighting, internal parasites, sickness, too low temperature and not eating. Always make sure that your turtle is eating right and that proper temperatures and lighting are maintained. If you are providing the appropriate care for your turtle and it is still not growing, then it may be suffering from sickness or intestinal parasites. Both are reasons you should go to a veterinarian for proper medical consultation.

Lack or Loss of Appetite

Some turtles have no problem eating while others may have an issue with it. A Mississippi map turtle won't eat when:

- It is sick
- It is stressed
- The other turtles around it are aggressively feeding
- The dietary items are not suitable
- The food is placed in the wrong place
- The habitat is too warm or too cold

Make sure that your turtle is eating the right kinds of food at the right amounts to maintain its health. Always check habitat temperatures and make it suitable for your Mississippi map turtle. You can spur your turtle to eat by trying a variety of live foods such as small fish, crickets and worms. If that doesn't work, try putting stick foods or pellets in small containers for them to munch on. If your turtle doesn't like a separate food container, place the food in the tank and see if it works. Make sure to clean the tank of plant and food waste after meal time to avoid the spread of salmonella. You should also consider whether your turtle likes to feed on land or in the water.

If you notice that it takes its food to the water before feeding on it, then it is aquatic and you know what to do to spur eating next time.

Another important thing you should remember is to give your turtle time to eat. There will be times that it will immediately grab the food, and there will be times that it will look around first before they eat. Some turtles are nervous eaters who don't like being watched while they feed. If your turtle still won't feed after you have tried a lot of options, then it may be nursing a health problem and you need to bring it to the vet.

Not Swimming

Mississippi map turtles are aquatic, so if your pet isn't swimming, then it's an indication that there's a problem. Not swimming usually telltales of respiratory infection or another illness that is worth looking into. IF your turtle is sick, it will stay lethargic and just bask or withdraw to its shell. Another reason your pet turtle won't swim could be the temperature of the water. Check to make sure that the temperatures are right. If your turtle isn't sick and the water temperatures are okay and yet it still doesn't swim, there could be a problem with aggression from the other turtles that live with it.

When your turtle feels harassed or stressed, it will stay out of the water. Observe your tank to see turtles' reactions and interaction with each other.

Not Basking

As with their water, turtles also like the temperatures of their basking areas to be just right. They won't feel safe it is too hot, so they will just stay in the water. Check to make sure that the temperatures are right. If they are and your Mississippi map turtle still doesn't bask, it could be as sign that it is nervous or shy with people. Often, there are nervous turtles who prefer to bask in solitude and won't do so when you are around. To test if it is nervous around you, leave them alone for a while then secretly take a peak. If you see your turtle is stretched out and basking, then you doesn't have to worry. It will soon adjust to having you around, or you can simply give it time and let it bask by itself. You don't have to be around it all the time anyway. But if you already did this and your turtle is still not basking, and it is not rectified by adjusting the temperatures, then consider that it may be suffering from an illness that needs attention. Be on the lookout for other symptoms that indicate sickness. Have a vet check your Mississippi map turtle right away.

Sleeping a Lot

If your Mississippi map turtle seems to sleep a lot more than usual, then it may be feeling cold. Make sure to check if the habitat temperatures are right. Raising them by 5° usually will make a difference and you will soon see your turtle swimming and basking as it should. If it still sleeps more than necessary or is withdrawn into its shell, check for symptoms of underlying illness and consult with a veterinarian.

Burns, Bites, Cuts and/or Scratches

If you notice burns, bites, cuts and/or scratches on your Mississippi turtle, you should check its habitat. There might be some changes you need to apply. A submersible heater that is placed in its habitat without guards can cause burn turtles that prefer to sit under them to stay warm. Heat lamps also do the same. On the other hand, more dominant turtles in the tank can aggressively bite and scratch the less aggressive turtles. Rocks and other tank decorations can also cut and scratch your pet turtle.

If you notice a burn on your Mississippi map turtle, do not remove the burned tissue. Allow it to dry as a scab — this will prevent possible infection. Just make sure that the cause of the burn is removed. The scab will slough off in a matter of time. For scratch and bite wounds, wash the injured part with clean water and disinfect with Betadine. You can apply antibiotic then make sure that the turtle stays dry for at least an hour. Put your turtle in a separate aquarium with clean water and proceed with the same treatment daily until the wound heals.

Eyes and Ears Problems

Aside from a turtle's shell, its eyes and ears serve as a looking glass into its physical medical issues and health. Some conditions are hard to identify while others will are an immediate telltale sign that something is wrong. Swollen, bleeding, puffy and crusty—these are just some conditions that will tell you that your turtle is suffering from a medical condition that needs your attention. Read on to find out more about problems with your Mississippi map turtle's eyes and ears and how to treat them when needed.

- Puffy, closed or swollen eyes are usually caused by poor water quality. When there are high concentrations of chlorine in the water, it can cause unfavorable reactions to your turtle. You will know if it is caused by the chemical when your turtle keeps its eye closed while swimming and rubs its eye and twitches its head while basking after a swim. The reaction could go away after a couple of hours, but if it doesn't, you need to change your water or de - chlorinate it. You should also check your filtration system to improve your water quality. Make sure to change your water frequently so that it won't cause infections to your pet turtle. Also, a puffy or swollen eye can also be caused by an injury—it could have scratched itself, gotten cut by something in the habitat, or injured by another turtle.

- Vitamin A deficiency is yet another reason for puffy, swollen eyes. Check your turtle's diet and add foods that are rich in vitamins or give it a supplement. Consult with your vet regarding a revamp in your pet's diet. Never use Vitamin A drops as it can be fatal to your pet turtle when given in high doses.

- Poked or scratched eyes would be common in a tank with more than one turtle. To treat the injury, you can apply non-steroidal eye medication twice a day, making sure that the turtle stays dry for at least 20 minutes after application. Keep your pet in quarantine with clean water until the injury heal to avoid complications. If the condition doesn't get better, get the proper medication and care from a veterinarian.

- Infection could also cause swelling and this requires proper attention. If your turtle's diet is good, the water is clean, and it has not been poked or scratched by other turtles, then you may be looking at a bacterial infection or a sickness that manifests in swollen eyes. Bring your Mississippi map turtle to the vet immediately.

- If your turtle has bloody eyes, there may be a bacterial infection and it can be protected with a non-steroidal eye ointment as it heals on its own. If the condition doesn't improve, it is always a good idea to bring your turtle to the vet.

- A turtle that has cloudy eyes may be suffering from a deficiency in Vitamin A or an injury. Your veterinarian may give you some eye drops to treat this.

- When lumps appear on the side of your Mississippi map turtle's head, there is ear abscess. It I s not always caused by your habitat. There are just bacteria in the air than can find its way inside your turtle's body and infect it. You can't prevent it but you can treat it with medication at home after your vet has made an incision along the lump and drains the fluid out. After this operation, you will have to keep your turtle quarantined in a dry container, with about an hour or so of swimming in clean water. A few days is all it need to return to its normal state and you can return it to its habitat.

Shell and Skin Problems

As with the turtle's eyes and ears, you can tell its condition by looking at its shell and skin. Following are common problems/illnesses that a Mississippi map turtle can suffer from:

- **Shell Rot.** A turtle can suffer from a wet shell rot or a dry shell rot. Wet scuds can form on the turtle's shell, caused by fungal or bacterial infection. A shell that has a cut, crack or lesion can easily become infected when it can't get completely dry. The wet scuds give off a bad smell, are whitish/yellowish in color and has a pussy discharge. If it doesn't get treated, your turtle can get septicemia. Dry scuds, on the other hand, are caused by injuries and poor water quality. They are minor compared to wet scuds and appear as white patches on your turtle's shell. The vet will give you systemic or topical medications that are effective in treating both kinds of scuds.

- **Mineral Deposit Buildup.** Not to be confused with shell rot, this condition is caused by hard water—water that contains heavy mineral deposits. The effect can be seen when your Mississippi map turtle sheds: it should have a white-to-white coating and no pitting. Otherwise, bacteria are present. Your turtle may have sores, smell bad and excessively shed skin. If this is the condition, the turtle should then be moved to quarantine and the infected aquarium should be cleaned and disinfected. A veterinarian can help you remove the scutes and apply medication. If your turtle's shell is bleeding, bring your pet to the vet immediately to avoid septicemia.

- **Holes in the Shell.** Dietary neglect, infection or wounds can cause holes to appear in your Mississippi map turtle's shell. You may even see holes that look like ulcers with blood coming out. To avoid this, make sure that your pet turtle gets the right diet, enjoys sufficient basking time and has proper lighting. When these adjustments are made, your turtle will heal on its own after some time. They may have superficial scars after the repair, but it won't be a problem.

- **Red or Pink Skin.** While red patches on the skin may indicate septicemia, it is not always the case. Some younger turtles will have pink or rust-colored skins. If the habitat's temperatures are adjusted and the skin condition becomes normal, then there is nothing to worry about.

- **Soft Shell.** A young turtle will naturally harden its shell as it grows. If it doesn't, you just need to change its diet and provide it with enough UVB light. Soft spots can appear on your Mississippi map turtle's shell if it is having dietary problems. It can also be a sign of fungal infection. Make sure that you give your turtle a diet that is rich in calcium. If the shell condition doesn't improve with diet and UVB light, bring your pet to the vet for medication.

- **Excessive Shedding. Like reptiles, turtles shed their skin.** But their skin will come off in slight, fine quantities that can hardly be seen. So when you notice large strands of skin on your pet turtle, it may be suffering from excessive shedding. This happen as a result of too warm water temperatures, over-feeding, infection or poor water quality. Make the necessary adjustments and your turtle will be back to normal.

Chapter Four: Fun Facts and Myths

A turtle is one of the cutest pets you can ever own. It is so easy to love. If you are a new owner, or you are considering getting a pet Mississippi map turtle, or you have been taking care of maps for years, here are some interesting and fun facts about this amazing reptile that will make you love it even more. This chapter, I'll give you some turtle facts and I'll also bust those turtle myths you've probably read or heard somewhere.

Fun Turtle Facts

- Turtles have been around for so long and have been evolving for more than 200 million years—way before mammals, birds and other reptiles such as snakes, lizards and crocodiles. The turtle's ancestors used to have teeth and they don't retract their heads into their shell. But the other characteristics are the same with the modern turtles you see today. Did you know that the oldest turtle ever recorded passed away when it was the ripe old age of 188 years old! That was Tu'iMalila from Tonga Island.

- Turtles do not have ears but they can hear. You heard that right, they aren't deaf creatures. Their internal ear bones allow them to hear through vibrations and these bones are covered with delicate flaps of skin.

- The shell of Mississippi map turtles, like most turtles, is a fusion of bones—60 different ones—and is part of the turtle's skeleton, including its spine and rib cage. This bony, cartilaginous body part is super sturdy and is often used by turtles as a shield to protect themselves from predators.

- Turtles make room for themselves to go inside their shells by exhaling air from their lungs. When they exhale, the give out a hissing sound.

- Turtles live in water but they breathe air on land. They also lay their eggs on land instead of underwater. They are *amniotes*.

- Most aquatic turtles live up to 30 to 50 years. Tortoises and box turtles can live up to 100 years!

- Like different breeds of dogs, turtles come with their own personalities. Most of them are shy and nervous, some are dominant and aggressive. Often, Mississippi map turtles don't like to be played with or watched while they are feeding. The apparent bashfulness of these lovable creatures is actually so cute. Look into their eyes and even when you see that they don't like to play with you, they still look so adorable.

- While caring for them can take up some time and effort on your pat, turtles are generally easy to maintain—you just feed them, make sure they have enough space to move then leave them alone to do their thing. What's more, you can take your pet turtle anywhere as they are so small and carrying them around wouldn't cause you any inconvenience.

- Your pet turtle will not hurt you. Even the most aggressive turtles raised in captivity will not deliberately hurt you. Turtles are generally harmless to humans—just don't get the snapping turtle, of course.

- You will become more responsible when you raise a pet turtle because you will learn to care for something that will depend on you. The same principle goes for any kind of pet you want to get.

- The Mississippi map turtle, like most pet turtles, will instantly be your best friend as soon as you bring it home! It may sound funny, but really, if you need someone to listen to you, your pet turtle will sit there and hear you out. You can even *shellebrate* your success with it (get the pun?).

If you don't want to feel alone, get a pet turtle—it is adorably good company and it is sure to stay with you a long, long time. And they won't run away. Well, even if they do get out of the enclosure, they won't get very far. So go and buy yourself a pet turtle!

Here is how to say "turtle" in different languages around the world:

- English: *Turtle, Tortoise*
- Arabic: *Fakroun*
- Chinese: *Gui, Wangba*
- French: *Tortue*
- Spanish: *Galápago, Tortuga*
- Japanese: *Kame*
- German: *Schildkröte*
- Italian: *Tartaruga*
- Polish: *Zolw*
- Czech: *Zelva*
  Portugese: *Tartaruga, Cagado*
- Russian: *Czerepakha*
- Dutch: *Schildpad*
- Filipino: *Pagong*
- Thai: *Tao*
- Swedish: *Sköldpadda*
- Greek: *Chelona*
- Turkish: *Kaplumbaga*
- Hindi: *Kacchua Tsalagi*
- Vietnamese: Danh tõ
- Indonesian: *Kura-kura*
- Afrikaans: *Skilpad*
- Zulu: *Ifutu*

Myths Surrounding Turtles

Everything comes with a myth and the same is true for turtles. There are so many misconceptions, legends and old wives' tales about them and about caring for them that people often think twice before getting turtles for pets. Hopefully, this section of the book will provide you some insight and learning.

Myth 1: When a turtle bites a person, it won't let go until it will hear thunder

It is quite entertaining, albeit scary, of course, for some people to hear this myth. Who would want to be bitten by a turtle and get stuck to it until thunder comes? However, this is a false legend. A turtle generally won't bite a person (unless it is a snapping turtle) and is quite harmless. But in the event it does bite someone or something, it will let go after a short while.

People often ask, "Do turtles bite?" If something has a mouth, you can bet your bottom dollar that it can bite! So if you feel like feeding your turtle by hand, then use tongs until it is already trained to eat from your hand. Most turtles will not have a very good aim and can accidentally bite you instead of their food target.

Myth 2: Turtles carry and can transmit salmonella to you.

This is both true and false. Yes, turtles are carriers of salmonella. It is part of their gut flora. But no, it cannot transmit salmonella to you just because you own one. However, just as eating eggs, pork and chicken can be a risk for being poisoned with salmonella, the same goes when you improperly handle your pet turtle. Learn more about proper handling of turtles in the other chapters of this book to avoid catching salmonella. Remember, for decades, there have been so many turtle keepers all over the world who have successfully taken care of different breeds of turtles and they never got ill from handling turtles.

Myth 3: A turtle's growth will be limited to the size of its habitat or enclosure.

A healthy turtle will grow to its full potential no matter the size of its enclosure. When it is provided with adequate food, the right habitat temperatures, and good quality water, you will soon find yourself needing a bigger enclosure to house your pet. When its growth is stunted, it can be caused by an underlying sickness or poor husbandry, but not because of the size of its home.

Myth 4: A turtle can leave its shell.

While it can be seen in most children's cartoon shows, a turtle can never get out of its shell. It is a part of its body and it will only leave the shell when it dies. The shell is part of a turtle's rib cage and they are attached to it. The turtle's shell will grow at the same rate as the rest of its body. You don't have to worry that your turtle will be too fat for its shell and might need a new one. As it grows, the shell may seem to come apart and this is normal. The turtle discards portions of its old shell and grows new segments. However, if the scutes of your pet turtle are coming off in large layers, or you see red spots in the areas where the scutes fell away, then have your turtle checked by a veterinarian.

Myth 5: It is not legal to own a turtle that is below 4 inches in length.

It depends on the species of turtle. If it is a protected species, yes it is illegal to own one. But if the species does not belong to a protected one, you can own or buy a turtle that is below 4 inches in shell length. Check with your state laws.

In the past, it didn't matter what species of turtle it is, a turtle below 4 inches is not allowed for sale as a pet because it was believed that it can cause salmonella poisoning. If you think about it, that rule is good for kids.

When they handle hatchling turtles, they can accidentally put the turtles in their mouths or rub their hands on their eyes. Small turtles can fit in the mouths of young children and yes, salmonella poisoning can happen, as well as the spread of other bacteria and germs. However, it is the parent's/adults' responsibility to watch over their children and not blame the turtle.

Myth 6: Baby turtles should be placed in shallow water until they grow and are able to swim well.

People think that baby turtles cannot swim well nor survive in deep waters. This is not true. Baby turtles have the same ability as grown turtles. Of course, this is dependent on their species. For instance, an adult mud turtle cannot swim or survive in deep waters. Other species could. When in the wild, they can find their way and thrive even in deep water and escape predators.

Myth 7: Turtles can eat pizza, hotdogs, ice cream and chocolate.

Yes they can. However, this doesn't mean that turtles should eat these junk foods. When both people and animals eat something that is not part of their regular diet, or when they overeat, they can get sick or have potentially bad health consequences.

Myth 8: When turtles have been kept in captivity in shallow water, they don't learn how to swim well and could drown when placed in deeper water.

Mississippi turtles are aquatic and won't have any problem swimming. They don't have to be taught, it is their nature. A healthy turtle will just naturally swim once it gets used to the depth of the water provided in its enclosure.

Myth 9: *Turtles are mean.*

Turtles are one of nature's most lovable, reserved creatures and are not aggressive towards people. But like any human or animal, they have a personality and temperament which can become aggressive when you pull them out of their habitat. Most turtles remain calm and docile when in water and won't even attempt to turn their heads at you or bite. If they feel you are trying to get them out of the water, then they will try to run away. Be careful not to put your hand in the water as they may think of your fingers as food. So you see, turtles are not mean, they just don't want to be mishandled or taken out of their comfort zones.

Myth 10: A hissing turtle is mad.

There are people and other animals that make a hissing sound when they are mad, but not turtles. When they hiss, they are afraid. Try breathing—when you inhale, your chest expands to pull air in and then release it by exhaling. It is different with a turtle's anatomy. Their chest cannot expand because they have a hard plastron. When they inhale, their lungs will expand inside their shell. When they are frightened, they will inhale making their shell so tight that they cannot pull their head and legs into hide, so turtles need to deflate their lungs by expelling air, causing the hissing sound. Once there is room for their head and legs to go into their shells, they will hide. So you see, they are not mad and warning you to stay away from them. They are actually hiding in fear.

Chapter Five: Mississippi Map Turtle Laws and Regulations

Other than the Mississippi map turtles, other species are native to Mississippi and are covered by Mississippi turtle laws. These include the following:

- Alabama Map Turtle
- Alabama Redbelly Turtle
- Alligator Snapping Turtle
- Black-knobbed Map Turtle
- Common Musk Turtle (Stinkpot)
- Common Snapping Turtle
- Eastern Box Turtle
- Eastern Chicken Turtle
- Eastern Mud Turtle
- Florida Cooter
- Gopher Tortoise
- Gulf Coast Smooth Softshell
- Gulf Coast Spiny Softshell
- Loggerhead Musk Turtle
- Midland Smooth Softshell
- Mississippi Diamondback
- Mississippi Map Turtle
- Mississippi Mud Turtle
- Ouachita Map Turtle
- Razorback Musk Turtle
- Ringed Map Turtle
- Red-eared Slider
- Stripeneck Musk Turtle
- Southern Painted Turtle
- Three-toed Box Turtle
- Western Chicken Turtle
- Yellow-blotched Map Turtle
- Yellowbelly Slider

Map Turtle Laws

There are different laws pertaining to possession of turtles, selling them commercially taking them from the wild that you need to be familiar with, if you want to own a pet turtle. Here they are in a nutshell:

I. Possession

a. It is legal to own a Mississippi map turtle and other turtle species that are not in the list of those considered illegal to own, transport, sell, or export such as the Alabama Red Belly, Gopher Tortoise, Yellow-blotched Sawback, Ringed Sawback or any Sea Turtle.

b. You can own a maximum of twenty reptiles but only four of the same species. That means you cannot have more than 4 Mississippi map turtles at home.

c. If you want to own an Alligator Snapping Turtle, you are only allowed to have one of it at a given time, with a minimum 24 - inch SCL.

d. It is illegal to possess, harvest, sell or transport turtle eggs.

e. It is illegal to buy, sell, offer to sell and barter any wild-caught reptiles.

f. There is no law regarding the regulation of non-native turtles. If you want to propagate native reptiles, you should secure a permit.

II. Commercial Laws

a. You can only export and import native reptiles when you have a permit. All animals that are to be imported and exported should originate outside of Mississippi or bought from someone who holds a permit for wildlife captive propagation.

b. Common Snapping Turtles may be caught and used for commercial purposes but only with the corresponding Snapping Turtle Permit and Commercial Fishing License. If you have permits, you do not have a limit on possession.

c. If you secure a Captive Propagation Permit, you can possess up to 8 animals of any species taken from the wild in Mississippi.

III. Taking Turtles from the Wild

a. Game hunting is allowed in small quantities. However, you will need to secure fishing or hunting license and the reptiles must be for your personal use and not for sale.

b. You cannot catch any of the turtles mentioned as illegal in Possession a

c. You can hunt for an Alligator Snapper only from July 1 to March 31.

Taking a Wild Turtle Home as a Pet

So you found a turtle in the wild and want to have it for a pet. Well, it is not a good decision. You should never bring a wild turtle home. First of all, you don't know what kind of species it is. And if you do know, the best course of action is to help it go where it is headed. An aquatic turtle would need to reach a body of water so help it get to the edge and allow them to get into the water at its own pace. Terrestrial turtles, on the other hand, will just need to go to underbrush near a forest. Remember, it is in the wild because it is a wild animal, so leave it there. If you really want a pet, go to a turtle pet store and get one.

Often people think that a turtle in the wild, especially a very tiny one (hatchling), is too small to survive. While they are extremely tiny when they hatch, young turtles can hide from predators and feed on insects. They are capable of surviving on their own and getting to the water or forest, wherever their natural habitat is. When you see one, help it a bit and wish it the best of luck in its adventure. Don't bring it home.

Another wrong belief is that a small turtle in the wild is looking for its mother. Unlike mammals, mothers of turtles don't care for their babies. After she lays the eggs, she goes back to her pond. Tiny hatchlings are independent and if you see one walking around, it is just looking for safety. You will hinder their journey when you pick them up and bring them home as a pet.

Others think that a turtle in the wild or those who happen to find its way into their yards is lost. Well, a turtle knows where it is and where it is going. The have strong instincts that help them locate the nearest body of water. Remember, they can thrive better in the wild.

Chapter Six: Petting and Training Your Mississippi Map Turtle

While it is advised not to handle your pet turtles too much, it largely depends on the personality and temperament of your pet as well as how you interact with it. It can be a bit tricky but it is not impossible. Here is a list of some advice on how you can pet your Mississippi map turtle without injuring or stressing it out:

Always approach your pet turtle from the front.

You never want to surprise a turtle because it can get frightened and bite your finger or hand. Allow it to see you first and be aware that you are trying to get close to it. This will put the pet turtle at ease and not consider you as a source of danger.

Always put them on a low, flat surface before petting them.

A turtle, as with any other pet, needs to feel safe before it can interact with anyone or anything. By putting them on the floor, they will feel secure and ready to mingle.

Start by petting the top of its head.

Very gently trace your finger on the top of your Mississippi map turtle's head. Try not to touch its' eyes and nose. If it stays still, it likes you petting its head. But if your turtle throws its head up in the air and its mouth is open while doing so, then it doesn't like what you are doing, so you need to stop. Don't let your turtle until it trusts you completely.

You can pet its cheeks and chin.

It is important that you already know that your turtle likes to be touched before you try this. Gently rub your finger under your pet map's chin and trace it along its cheeks.

Make massaging motions on its neck.

A turtle that trusts you, and is used to your touches, will allow you to massage its neck.

Pet the shell.

As it is part of its body, your pet turtle can feel your touch on its shell. You can make slow circular strokes or trace straight lines gently along its shell.

Use a soft-bristled toothbrush to rub the shell.

Instead of using your fingers, try brushing the bristles of a toothbrush along the length of your pet turtle's shell.

Enjoy lap time.

If it doesn't like to be touched, you can let your pet turtle sit or crawl on your lap. Be warned, though, that turtles often urinate once they are picked up so be careful when put them on your body.

It is important to remember that your pet will not always be receptive to your touch and doesn't want to be petted all the time. Just be patient and persistent. The more you handle your turtle, gently, it will grow to trust you and be more responsive to human interaction. Usually, turtles see their human keepers as a food source. You can encourage it to enjoy petting by rewarding it with food or treats.

Who says you can't train a turtle? One they trust you and are used to your handling and petting, you can take the next step and train your Mississippi map turtle. Again, how you behave towards your turtle will be a big factor on how they respond to you. If they don't trust you, they will just see you as someone who provides their food. Following is a list of things you can do to keep your turtle at ease before you try training it:

Give it a name.

Don't be surprised, but like other pets, turtles can understand their names. If you name your pet turtle, it will signify that you acknowledge it and it will feel that it can trust you to be good to it. Moreover, it knows when and how to respond to you, when you call it by name.

Call it by name whenever you see it.

Your turtle will appreciate being called by name instead of simply nothing. As they get used to you calling them by name, they will look at you whenever you call them and listen to what you have to say.

Take time to play with them.

Simple playing can be the foundation of your training. One game you can play with your pet turtle is to let it follow something around. Gently roll something at it, it will get curious and go near the object to sniff it. Take it away and roll it to another side. Your turtle will follow it out of curiosity. You can also play "hide-a-treat" where your turtle will hunt for a treat you hid and eat it as a reward. Whatever game you play with your turtle, the idea is to spend time with it.

Pet your turtle.

As with the advices given above, you need to pet your turtle so that it can grow in its responsiveness to your interactions. This will make it easy to teach your turtle to do other things.

Feed your turtle by hand.

Hand feeding creates a special bonding moment between you and your pet turtle. However, you should only try to feed by hand when you are sure that your turtle has practiced its aim.

Before you can hand feed, you must train your turtle by developing a routine. Feed your turtle by placing food it its enclosure at the same time every day. This way it will get used to the routine. Stay to watch while it eats and make very minimal, slow movements so it will know you are there but not actually disturbing it. Then you can proceed to gradual hand feeding. Hold a leaf of lettuce about 6 inches away from your pet and patiently wait for it to come to you and eat. You can also try to hold crickets or other live foods using tongs to get your pet's interest. The living food will keep your turtle's attention from your hand and encourage it to feed. Soon it will get used to having your hand in the way.

Allow your pet to explore around your home.

Your pet turtle is not just a display for people to gawk at. You need to make it feel like they are a part of your life, a part of your family. You can let it roam around your house, just make sure that you set the right boundaries. Watch it go and when it has gone a distance away from you, try to call its name and see if it stops to turn around. Have a treat ready for it when it does. You can practice this lot of times. Soon, you will have your turtle coming back to you when you call it.

Repetition is key.

When you are training your pet to do something, you should do it over and over again. You can teach it to follow voice commands or signals so it do the following tricks: climb up on your hand, nod its head or shake your hand. You can even go as far as asking your turtle to pick something up and give it back to you.

Give your turtle a safe zone.

Provide a spot for your turtle to hide when it feels like hiding and never invade that safe zone. A safe zone can be a log, a cave or a shelter house. It will help your pet turtle manage stress and feel safe from threat. It will also be a calming place for it. By staying away from it when it is hiding or resting, your turtle will not feel harassed. When your turtle observes that you are not invading its safe zone, then it will not consider you a threat and start to trust you.

The most important tip is to always show your pet turtle that you care for it. Talk with it even as you feed it. You can even sing to it. Loving them is more than just feeding them. Regularly observe when you are connecting with your pet turtle. You will discover when it is active, when it doesn't like something, what scares it, and when it makes positive interaction. As you observe it, your turtle will also become accustomed to your presence as a person and not a food source. Make sure you limit your interactions until your Mississippi map turtle voluntarily socializes with you. Treat them as a friend and they will respond to you as a friend.

These tips are here to help you improve your connection with your pet, not just to be able to teach them tricks so you can show them off. Your relationship with your pet is the most important thing.

Chapter Seven: What to Do in Different Turtle Situations

Usually, you can find an injured turtle by a roadside. It may be crossing the road and if it's a busy one, then the turtle's journey often ends in that same road. If you see a turtle on the road, check to see if it is still alive. Don't assume that it is already dead just because it is staying still. You cannot tell the extent of its injuries so it is better to bring it to an emergency wildlife center. Who knows, the turtle you save may be carrying eggs that can be rescued even if the mother is gravely injured. And even if a turtle is has suffered mortal injuries, be kind and get them off the street.

To transport injured turtles, you may need a box that is layered with a damp towel. It is best to keep them in a dark and cool place so it will stay calm while you transport it. Do not think that just because a turtle is an aquatic animal, you can transport it in water. The turtle can drown. Make sure you handle the injured turtle as slightly as possible. Too much handling can bring stress to an already injured turtle and it may bite you.

If you find yourself regularly helping and rescuing turtles, then it is best to keep a turtle kit handy. It should include the following:

- Sturdy transportation box (can be a folded down box, so it is easy to carry around)
- Old towel or paper towels
- Bottled water to be used to moisten your towels
- Latex gloves or leather gloves for handling
- Hand sanitizer

Turtle Adoption

Thinking about adopting a turtle instead of buying a hatchling? Great! A lot of people are so excited in the beginning but they jump into the husbandry without giving it careful thought and proper research. They end up making care errors then giving up their pet turtles. There are many abandoned pet turtles all over the country and they need interested people like you to give them new homes.

Turtle Rescue League offers a variety of pet turtles; including the Mississippi map turtle, as well as corresponding care sheets to help you prepare for being a turtle parent. If you are decided on adopting one, contact them right away and bring your new friend home.

Moving to a New Place

You don't have to leave your turtle behind if you are moving to a new home. As with any pet, your turtle can be part of all your life's journeys. You can safely transport your Mississippi map turtle via plane or car. You can also leave them in foster homes in case you will only be away for a set period of time.

Transporting by Car

As with rescuing injured turtles, use a turtle kit. Make sure your transportation box is sturdy, dry and opaque. You don't want your turtle to be housed in a cold, wet box. An opaque container will also help your turtle be less stressed.

The box should just be slightly bigger than your pet turtle because it will find tight spaces rather comforting. If the box is too big, the turtle will move around and want a way out.

Put four to six ¼-inch holes at the top of your cardboard box. This allows for enough air and still keeps the inside of the box dark. Line it with a dry kitchen towel to serve as a cushion. Place the turtle and cover it with an additional towel. Close the lid. You can tape it as necessary.

If you are using an opaque plastic container, moisten a kitchen towel with water and layer it on the bottom so that the turtle can have enough cushion and humidity. Place the turtle in and cover it with a dry towel. Close the lid and use tape if the plastic container doesn't have a lock. Most plastic storage containers already have holes for air.

On the day you will move, make sure to keep your turtle in a quiet place after boxing it up. Your turtle transportation box should be the last item to be loaded on your car and the first one to be unloaded. This will make sure that the turtle is not exposed to extreme cold or heat. The turtle will most likely nap during your trip so try not to disturb him by checking inside the box every so often.

Transporting by Air

Turtles can be transported via place. Check the live animal policies from different shipping options (UPS, DeltaDash or FEDEX). Important tip: do not ship near a holiday so the turtle doesn't have a long travel period and always check the weather so you can avoid exposing your turtle to adverse weather conditions, extreme temperatures. It is best to ship at the beginning of the week.

Temporary Fostering

Seasonal jobs, extended vacations and other temporary moves should not be a reason to give up your pet. You can ask family or friends to look out for your turtle while you are away. This temporary set-up will not affect your turtle greatly.

Can't Take Care of Your Turtle Anymore?

The time may come when you cannot take care of your turtle anymore and there is one very important thing you need to remember: do not ever release your Mississippi map turtle back into the wild. When you think about it, you won't even consider leaving your pet dog or cat into the wild. Just because a turtle naturally lives in the wild doesn't mean it is the perfect spot for you to leave it. You may think there are other turtles in that pond or river and the turtle can get enough water, sunlight and food. But it's just not ideal, especially if your turtle has been raised in captivity. All or most of its life, it wouldn't know how to hunt for food, and it has lived in a regulated environment. It can also catch a disease that can go unchecked, which could have been managed in a captive environment. Given these, your pet turtle will have a small chance of survival and may even cause damage to other animals native to where you will leave it.

If you have no choice but to re - home your turtle, consider finding organizations that facilitate adoption. Find online forums and internet groups that you can connect with to help you locate a suitable new family for your pet map. You can also check on your local pet store and they might consider buying your Mississippi map turtle or let you make an announcement on their community board for possible adoption.

The decision to get a pet, no matter what kind of animal it is, is something that you should give careful consideration. You can't just turn your back when the going gets tough. When you choose an animal to call your own, give it all you've got and be prepared to care for it in the long run.

Photo Credits

Page 1 Photo by user Peter Paplanus via Flickr.com,

https://www.flickr.com/photos/2ndpeter/19034948469/

Page 6 Photo by user Scott Penner via Flickr.com,

https://www.flickr.com/photos/penner/4289274890/

Page 18 Photo by user Scott Penner via Flickr.com,

https://www.flickr.com/photos/penner/4504679626/

Page 45 Photo by user Scott Penner via Flickr.com,

https://www.flickr.com/photos/penner/4504043781/

Page 69 Photo by user Scott Penner via Flickr.com,

https://www.flickr.com/photos/penner/4504037129/

Page 81 Photo by user bgv23 via Flickr.com,

https://www.flickr.com/photos/panamapictures/4140191962/

Page 87 Photo by user Peter Paplanu via Flickr.com,

https://www.flickr.com/photos/2ndpeter/19034948469/

Page 96 Photo by user Andrew Hoffman via Flickr.com,

https://www.flickr.com/photos/71701055@N00/7513841728/

References

10 Common Myth Tortoises – Reptile Expert

http://www.reptileexpert.co.uk/common-myths-turtles-tortoises.html

42 CFR 71.52 - Turtles, tortoises, and terrapins – Cornell Law School

https://www.law.cornell.edu/cfr/text/42/71.52

Caring for Pet Mississippi Map Turtles – The Spruce.com

https://www.thespruce.com/mississippi-map-turtles-1238353

Mississippi Map Turtle – Austin's Turtle Page

http://www.austinsturtlepage.com/Care/caresheet-mississippi_map.htm

Mississippi Map Turtle – PetGuide.com

http://www.petguide.com/breeds/turtle/mississippi-map-turtle/

Mississippi Map Turtles Care Sheet – Reptile Centre

https://www.reptilecentre.com/info-mississippi-map-turtle-care-sheet

Mississippi Map Turtle - Graptemys pseudogeographica kohni – PetMD.c

https://www.petmd.com/reptile/species/mississippi-map-turtle

Top 10 Weird Turtle Facts – Animal Planet

http://www.animalplanet.com/tv-shows/call-of-the-wildman/lists/10-weird-turtle-facts/

Turtles and Tortoises Facts – Drs. Foster & Smith Education

https://www.drsfostersmith.com/pic/article.cfm?articleid=828

Turtle Facts – LiveScience.com

https://www.livescience.com/52361-turtle-facts.html

www.ingramcontent.com/pod-product-compliance
Lightning Source LLC
Chambersburg PA
CBHW062006040426
42447CB00010B/1930